WHAT MAKES A REMBRANDT
A REMBRANDT?

Richard Mühlberger

The Metropolitan Museum of Art
Viking
NEW YORK

VIKING
Published by the Penguin Group, Penguin Putnam Books for Young Readers, 345 Hudson Street, New York, New York 10014.

Paperback edition published in 1993 by The Metropolitan Museum of Art and Viking, a division of Penguin Books USA Inc.
Hardcover edition published in 2002 by The Metropolitan Museum of Art and Viking, a division of Penguin Putnam Books for Young Readers.

10 9 8 7 6 5 4 3 2 1

Produced by the Department of Special Publications, The Metropolitan Museum of Art: Series Editor, Mary Beth Brewer; Cover Design, Anna Raff; Design, Nai Y. Chang.

The Library of Congress has cataloged the paperback edition as follows:

Mühlberger, Richard. What makes a Rembrandt a Rembrandt? / Richard Mühlberger.
p. cm.
"The Metropolitan Museum of Art."
Summary: Explores such art topics as style, composition, color, and subject matter as they relate to twelve works by Rembrandt.
ISBN 0-87099-675-4 (MMA pbk.) ISBN 0-670-85199-X (Viking pbk.)
1. Rembrandt Harmenszoon van Rijn, 1606–1669—Criticism and interpretation—Juvenile literature. 2. Painting, Dutch—Juvenile literature. 3. Painting, Modern—17th–18th centuries—Netherlands—Juvenile literature. [1. Rembrandt Harmenszoon van Rijn, 1606–1669. 2. Painting, Dutch. 3. Art appreciation.] I. Metropolitan Museum of Art (New York, N.Y.) II. Title.
ND653.R4M783 1993 759.9492—dc20 93-7581 CIP AC

ISBN 1-55839-051-9 (MMA) ISBN 0-670-03572-6 (Viking)

Printed in Italy

ILLUSTRATIONS

Unless otherwise noted, all works are by Rembrandt van Rijn and in oil on canvas.

Pages 1 and 2: *Woman with a Pink*, 36¼ x 29⅜ in., The Metropolitan Museum of Art, Bequest of Benjamin Altman, 1913, 14.40.622.

Page 6: *Self-Portrait Leaning on a Stone Sill*, etching, 8 5/16 x 6⅝ in., The Metropolitan Museum of Art, H. O. Havemeyer Collection, Bequest of Mrs. H. O. Havemeyer, 1929, 29.107.25.

Page 8: *The Artist in His Studio*, oil on panel, 9¾ x 12½ in., Zoë Oliver Sheman Collection, Given in memory of Lillie Oliver Poor, Courtesy, Museum of Fine Arts, Boston.

Page 11: Thomas de Keyser, *The Anatomy Lesson of Dr. Sebastian Egbertszoon*, 53⅛ x 73¼ in., 1619, Amsterdams Historisch Museum.

Page 12: *The Anatomy Lesson of Dr. Tulp*, 66¾ x 85¼ in., 1632; photograph, © Mauritshuis, The Hague, inv. nr. 146.

Page 17: *Man in Oriental Costume (The Noble Slav)*, 60⅛ x 43¾ in., 1632, The Metropolitan Museum of Art, Bequest of William K. Vanderbilt, 1920, 20.155.2.

Page 18: *Storm on the Sea of Galilee*, 63 x 50⅜ in., 1633, Isabella Stewart Gardner Museum, Boston.

Page 23: *Flora*, 49⅛ x 39½ in., 1634, The Hermitage, St. Petersburg; photograph, Scala/Art Resource, New York.

Page 24: *Belshazzar's Feast*, 65¾ x 82¼ in., reproduced by courtesy of the Trustees, The National Gallery, London.

Page 29: *Anslo and His Wife*, 69¼ x 82⅝ in., 1641, © Bildarchiv Preußischer Kulturbesitz, Berlin, 1993; photograph, Jörg P. Anders.

Page 32: *The Night Watch*, 143½ x 172½ in., 1642, Rijskmuseum-Foundation, Amsterdam.

Page 39: *Aristotle with a Bust of Homer*, 56½ x 53¾ in., 1653, The Metropolitan Museum of Art, Purchased with special funds and gifts of friends of the Museum, 1961, 61.198.

Page 40: *Jacob Blessing the Sons of Joseph*, 69⅛ x 82⅞ in., 1656, Staatliche Museen, Kassel.

Page 42: *Self-Portrait*, 31⅝ x 26½ in., 1660, The Metropolitan Museum of Art, Bequest of Benjamin Altman, 1913, 14.40.618.

Page 44: *Man with a Magnifying Glass*, 36 x 29¼ in., The Metropolitan Museum of Art, Bequest of Benjamin Altman, 1913, 14.40.621.

Page 45: *Woman with a Pink*, 36¼ x 29⅜ in., The Metropolitan Museum of Art, Bequest of Benjamin Altman, 1913, 14.40.622.

Page 47: *The Three Trees*, etching with drypoint and burin, 8⅛ x 10 15/16 in., The Metropolitan Museum of Art, H. O. Havemeyer Collection, Bequest of Mrs. H. O. Havemeyer, 1929, 29.107.31.

Page 49: *The Syndics of the Clothmakers' Guild*, 75⅜ x 109¾ in., Rijksmuseum-Foundation, Amsterdam.

CONTENTS

SELF-PORTRAIT LEANING ON A STONE SILL

Meet Rembrandt van Rijn

Rembrandt Harmenszoon van Rijn was born on July 15, 1606, in the prosperous town of Leiden in Holland. Leiden was famous for its university, the oldest in the Netherlands. Rembrandt's father, the half owner of a mill, saved enough money to send his son to college after he finished seven years at the local Latin School. Rembrandt was then about fourteen years old.

It is not known when or how Rembrandt learned about art, but he was sure enough of his interest in it to ask his father if he could study painting. He dropped out of college after only a few months and spent the next three years training with a painter in Leiden. At the time, Italian art was the model for Dutch artists. Rembrandt was lucky because his teacher knew Italy's greatest art from the many years he had lived and traveled there.

Rembrandt continued his art studies with Pieter Lastman, a popular and successful painter who had also studied in Italy. After only six months, Rembrandt had absorbed his master's lessons. He was ready to begin his own life as an artist.

Although his teachers were sophisticated travelers, Rembrandt preferred to stick close to home. When asked why he did not go to Italy to learn about the latest painting styles and techniques as other artists did, Rembrandt said he was too busy. Throughout his entire life, the artist never journeyed very far from the familiar place where he was born.

Rembrandt's teachers got their style from Italy, and they passed it on to Rembrandt. He accepted some of it, but preferred to find his own inspiration in the world he knew.

By the time he was twenty-three years old, Rembrandt's fame had spread beyond his hometown and he was the proud master of an ambitious studio.

The Artist in His Studio

Rembrandt is ready to paint. Facing him is a huge panel with its clean surface reflecting the light of a bright Dutch day. The young artist will spend a few minutes thinking about what the finished painting will look like. An image of it has probably been forming in his imagination for days, or even weeks, in preparation for this moment. Once he can see it complete in his mind's eye, he will walk across the wood plank floor, lift the brush in his hand, and begin.

To put distance between the image of himself and the panel, which rests on a sturdy easel, Rembrandt exaggerated perspective. As the floorboards recede to the far wall, they become smaller. The dark shadows the easel casts on the floor and the lines that indicate where the floor meets the walls also help measure the span between the young artist and his painting-to-be. Rembrandt wanted himself to appear small and the wood panel large. Perhaps it was his way of saying how important this work was to him.

Chiaroscuro

The front of the panel in Rembrandt's studio catches sunshine that floods through the large windows off to the left. But the back of the panel, the only part that can be seen in the painting, is hidden from the light. The panel casts a shadow that slants across the door behind the easel. Light from the windows also touches the front of Rembrandt's body. Behind him, in the shaded corner of the room, the jug, bottle, and pan on his worktable are barely visible.

Rembrandt liked strong contrasts of light and dark and used them in his paintings all his life, letting darkness hide unnecessary details while using light to bring figures and objects out from the shadows. The high contrast of light against dark changed an ordinary scene into a dramatic one. In this painting, the easel and its blank panel would not seem as large if the back were brightly lighted like the front, nor would Rembrandt seem as small if he were standing fully in the sun. His teachers probably taught him the Italian word for this use of light and dark, chiaroscuro. *Chiaro* means light, and *scuro* means dark.

Rembrandt's Costumes

Almost thirty years after he completed this painting, Rembrandt made a drawing of himself standing in his studio that shows that he still liked to wear hats and long garments when he

With a few brief marks of the brush, Rembrandt described his hands and cloaked his face in shadow. The tools he holds are painted distinctly enough to identify: brushes, a palette on which he will mix his paints, and a maulstick. This latter device has a padded end to hold against the canvas. The hand that is painting rests on the stick while doing detailed work.

worked. One of his pupils reported that he dressed in dirty old clothes stained with paint from wiping his brushes on them. But the costume he wears here as a young man seems too fine for that kind of treatment. If he starts to paint in it, he probably will not do so for long, for the dangling sleeves are sure to get in his way. The robe, called a tabard, was old-fashioned by the time Rembrandt was alive. A short tabard was part of the costume of a knight in armor. Rembrandt collected numerous rich and exotic costumes that he kept in his studio for models to wear for the biblical and historical scenes he painted. Many such costumes, perhaps including the robe he wears in this scene, can be spotted in his paintings.

Rembrandt's studio was on the second floor of a once-grand house. Although the building was probably not much older than he was, the cracked plaster behind his easel and over the door indicates that it had fallen into neglect. The room had a fireplace to warm Rembrandt on the damp days that are common in Holland. The door behind the easel opened onto a stairway to the front hall and the street beyond. Although solitary in this painting, Rembrandt was not alone in his studio very often. He may have shared it with another artist and he had three students during his last four years in Leiden. The two clean palettes hanging from a nail in the far wall are a clue that this almost vacant space may have been used by others.

Praise from a Visitor

An important visitor came to Rembrandt's studio in 1629, the year he painted himself before his easel. He was Constantijn Huygens, the secretary to three successive princes of the House of Orange, the noble family who led the Netherlands to independence from Spain. Huygens was one of the most powerful and best-educated men in Holland, and he liked Rembrandt's work. He described the artist as looking more like a smooth-faced boy than a man, adding that he "likes to concentrate on smaller paintings," and that they were more effective than "the colossal canvases of others." But when Huygens saw a large painting by Rembrandt during his visit, he felt it surpassed everything in art that had ever been produced. "Bravo, Rembrandt!" Huygens wrote.

An Important Commission

When Constantijn Huygens told his friends about Rembrandt, they began to buy his work. In 1631, Rembrandt moved to Amsterdam, a large city with more opportunity for portrait commissions.

Thomas de Keyser
THE ANATOMY LESSON OF DR. SEBASTIAN EGBERTSZOON

Although Thomas de Keyser enlivened his composition by varying the gestures, this picture remains a more traditional anatomy lesson painting than Rembrandt's.

Rembrandt was asked by Dr. Nicholaes Tulp to paint the doctor's annual anatomy lesson. The work would commemorate Tulp's term as a professor of anatomy at Amsterdam's Surgeons Guild. Rembrandt understood the importance of such paintings; it was a tradition for every anatomy professor to commission one.

Traditional Anatomy Lesson Paintings

Anatomy lessons were public events, and people paid to get into the theater where they were held. The lessons were not painted the way they actually occurred, because there were too many people present and too much confusion. Artists usually lined up the doctors in rows and showed them all staring straight ahead. The results usually looked formal and unexciting.

The Anatomy Lesson of Dr. Tulp

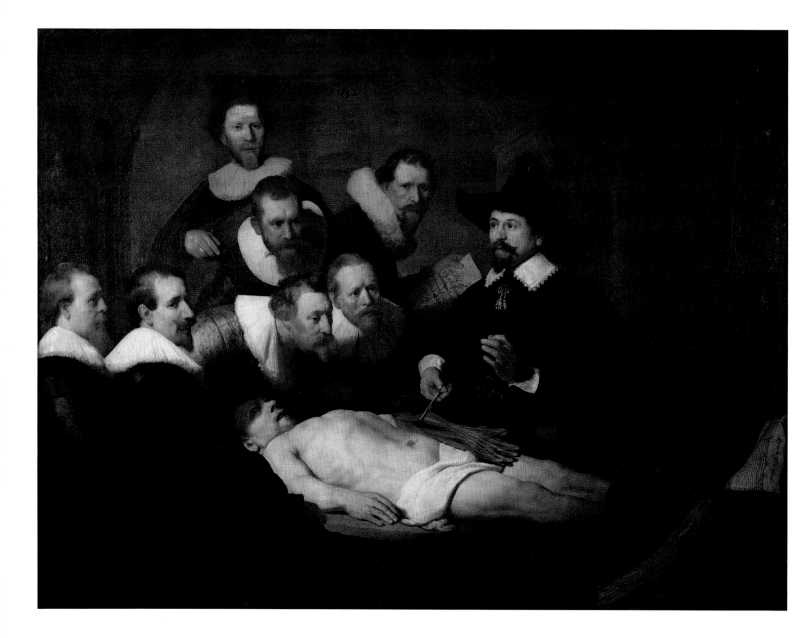

A Pyramid of Physicians

Rembrandt did not like that idea. He wanted to enliven the group portrait, so he arranged his distinguished subjects in a pyramid and turned each one's head differently, from the one in profile on the far left to the head facing forward at the top. The cadaver is placed diagonally. Rembrandt's innovative composition made the men look like vital, intelligent individuals.

An arc of shadow sweeps around the group, and the black garments of the two men on the left blend in with it. The darkness emphasizes the skin of the corpse and the faces of the members of the Surgeons Guild. This contrast is caused by strong light coming into the anatomy theater from the left.

Rembrandt was asked to include seven gentlemen in his painting, along with Dr. Tulp and the corpse. The man whose head is closest to Dr. Tulp's holds a list with the names of all the men on it. Tulp was famous and told Rembrandt exactly how he wanted himself presented, but the young artist was left to decide how everything else was going to look.

The dead man was a twenty-eight-year-old criminal named Adriaen, known familiarly as The Kid. He had been hanged for his crimes the day before Dr. Tulp began the dissection of his body. In the painting, the great anatomy expert has opened Adriaen's hand and arm and is holding the flexor muscles with a metal forceps. With his own forearm, Tulp demonstrates how the flexor muscles cause the fingers to bend. In actual practice at the time, doctors began dissections by opening the chest, but here the professor chose to feature the hand because it had long been considered the supreme instrument of human beings, the feature that set them apart from the animals. The hand was also the chief tool of both surgeons and painters.

Dr. Nicholaes Tulp, born thirteen years before Rembrandt, was a medical doctor in Amsterdam. He was appointed public lecturer of the Surgeons Guild in 1628, recognition that his knowledge of anatomy was the most modern in all of Holland. Rembrandt warmed Tulp's face with red tones, causing it to stand out from the brown, black, and white surroundings.

Dr. Tulp's sensitive hands stand out against his black costume, and he is dressed differently from all his colleagues. His dramatic hat and simple collar highlight the saintly look on his face. It was a custom to start an anatomy lesson with the exhortation "Know thyself," for the Dutch believed that they could come to understand God through the study of his creations, of which the human body was a part. Tulp was their guide. He has the rapt attention of two colleagues, while his words prompt another two to study the anatomy book at Adriaen's feet. The man on the far left seems to pay little attention to the lesson, and the man holding the list of names looks startled as he gazes out at the viewers of the painting. At the top of the pyramid, another man looks out, his hand pointed at poor Adriaen. Perhaps the artist is using the cadaver to remind viewers that everyone's life will eventually end. Such a painting is called a *memento mori*, which means "Remember, you will die."

The Anatomy Lesson of Dr. Tulp made Rembrandt famous. He decided to stay in Amsterdam, where portrait commissions poured into his new studio. They did not cease for twenty years.

Anatomy lessons took place during winter in an unheated theater, to lessen the chance of the corpse decaying before the lesson was over. Rembrandt contrasts Dr. Tulp's strong and skillful hands with the bloodless cadaver's muscle and cartilage.

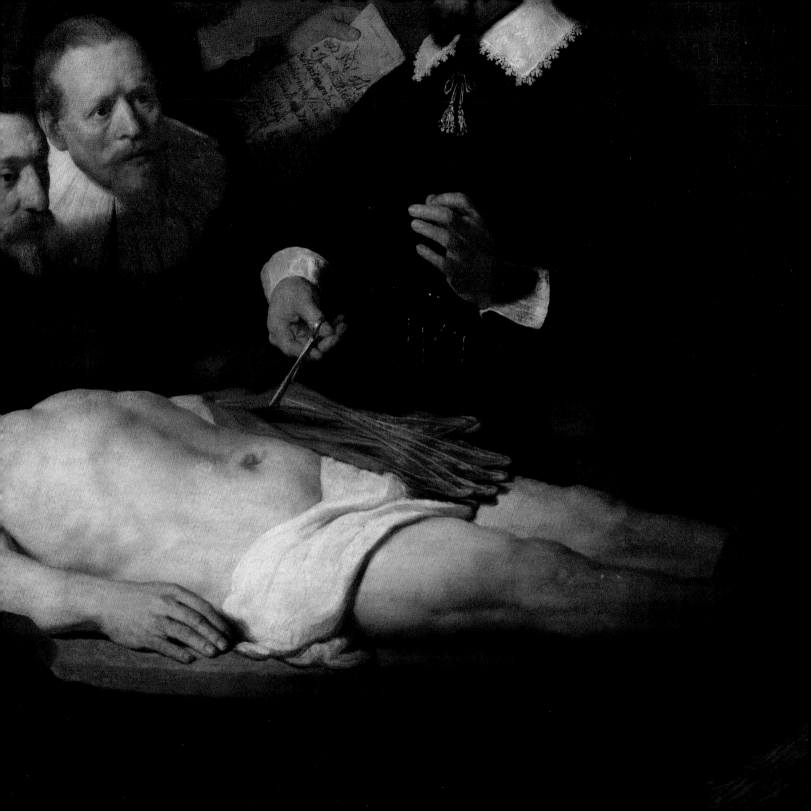

Man in Oriental Costume

In the seventeenth century, many travelers from Persia, Turkey, and other distant cities came to Amsterdam. The port city had become the busiest in Europe, and foreign delegations arrived to arrange trading agreements and to see the world's richest city. Rembrandt had sketched these visitors, but when he painted *Man in Oriental Costume*, he did not depend on them for inspiration. Instead, he turned to the assortment of costumes he had been collecting.

A Bagful of Tricks

Just as Rembrandt had a trunkful of costumes to turn his models into exotic characters, he also had a bagful of tricks to keep a simple painting from becoming dull. In this painting, one trick was positioning the model slightly to the left of the canvas's center. One of his elbows thrusts out, the other back, yet the twist of the body that results does not prevent the subject from looking straight ahead.

Rembrandt also created interest by the way he lighted the painting. A single source of light comes from the upper left and hits the man's right side, while his left side is largely in shadow. In the background, however, it is just the opposite. Behind the man's right side there is shadow, and light glows behind his left side.

Light areas stand out against darkness, and shadowy areas against light. This use of light makes the figure seem bold and dignified, and it emphasizes the outline he cuts against the backdrop.

The cloak is painted in shades of yellow and brown to give the impression of heavy gold fabric. As this rich textile sweeps over the model's right arm, it catches enough bright light to reveal floral patterns. Brown fur trims the majestic garment. A scarf of silk, with green-blue and light yellow embroidery, is loosely draped around the man's shoulders. The end of it, hanging down his chest, is embellished with gold threads, and more gold hangs nearby in a large pendant showing the crescent moon, a symbol of Islam. The man wears two pearl earrings, and the fabric in the ballooning turban is held in place by two jewels.

Rembrandt learned to lavish attention on small parts of a painting, leaving the rest without much detail. He knew that details look more impressive surrounded by areas that are plain; they are harder to notice when they cover the entire surface of a painting. Here, the right side and bottom of the cloak lack precise detail, yet it is easy to imagine that they are as fine as the areas Rembrandt describes more fully elsewhere.

The model for this painting was probably a Dutchman. By dressing a Dutch model in exotic clothing, Rembrandt made the strange and foreign seem less unusual.

The Dutch knew ships, so the sails and riggings in Rembrandt's turbulent seascape probably were scrutinized before the story became apparent. To a sea captain, a cross on the windwhipped flag atop the mast would have been the first clue that this is a scene from the New Testament. The painting combines "portraits" of the sea, the sky, a boat, and the passengers under stress.

Storm on the Sea of Galilee

Two Paintings in One

In the mid-seventeenth century, everyone in Holland seemed to want paintings. Peter Mundy, an English visitor to the Lowlands in 1640, wrote that even blacksmiths and cobblers "will have some picture or other by their forge and in their stall." A Dutch artist chose a specialty when he was young. He stuck to it and did not paint other kinds of subjects. Thus, a portrait painter ordinarily did not paint landscapes, nor would a landscape painter illustrate a story from history. There were flower painters, painters of birds, painters of towns, and many more kinds of specialists. Rembrandt's first teacher, for example, was a specialist in scenes of Hell. By becoming the best in one type of painting, an artist was almost guaranteed a regular income from sales. Painters, therefore, worked hard to excel in their chosen subject.

Rembrandt had two specialties, portraits and history paintings, but he also painted a few landscapes. *Storm on the Sea of Galilee* is a seascape, a kind of scene popular with the sea-faring Dutch and the only one that Rembrandt ever painted. At the same time, it is a religious painting, illustrating a well-known story from the New Testament.

During a ferocious storm, the disciples of Jesus were full of fear. As the waves threatened their ship, their master slept. When the disciples finally awakened him, Jesus commanded the storm to stop and admonished his followers as "Ye of little faith."

Rembrandt pictures a miracle about to take place on board the battered boat. He also shows the hopeless exertions of the men to survive the anger of the waves. Dutchmen knew the story from reading the Bible, and they also knew boats and the sea. How appreciative they must have been of the drama Rembrandt added to the simple New Testament tale.

The mast of the ship points toward two far corners of the painting. Extending an invisible line between them divides the canvas into a pair of triangles. Once again, Rembrandt used light to add drama to the picture. The left triangle is full of it, so that the force and size of the crashing wave can be seen. Much of the right triangle is filled with the surging brine and ominous sky. Matthew wrote that "the boat was being swamped by the waves." Rembrandt's water does just what the Bible describes. In addition, it lifts the prow of the vessel high into the sky. In seconds the ship will crash down into the unfriendly sea. The only hint that there is hope for the boat is the beautiful yellow light that opens gloriously in the distance, drenching the edge of the clouds and the ship's mainsail.

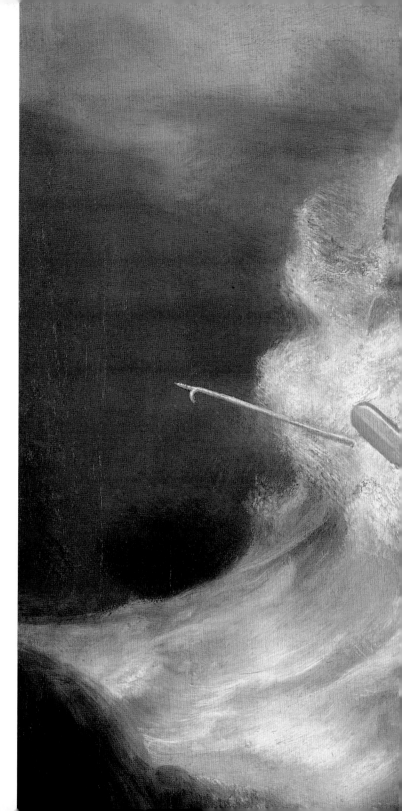

"Peace! Be Still!"

Rembrandt stressed the wickedness of the waves by showing their effect on the men in the boat. They are the twelve disciples of Jesus, among them sailors and fishermen. But all of them are as powerless as the broken riggings, the torn sail, and the useless rudder. The best they can do is hang on. One becomes sick over the side, and the man on the left clamps one hand to his hat and the other to a rigging stay. Rembrandt has given this man his own face. For an artist to include a self-portrait in a historical scene was not unusual; it was like saying, "Believe what you see. I was there, if only in my imagination."

Jesus is shown in a deep blue robe with rays of light behind his head. A disciple has grabbed his cloak and asks, "Teacher, do you not care if we perish?" Jesus immediately rebukes the wind and calls to the sea, "Peace! Be still!" Then he asks his disciples, "Where is your faith?"

The rays of light surrounding Jesus's head are a traditional religious symbol. They illuminate his pale face, causing it to contrast with his richly colored robes and the dark hull of the boat where he has been sleeping. The head of Jesus was to become a favorite subject of Rembrandt later in his career, but for now he is more interested in the story of Jesus's miracle.

Flora

Good Fortune

Since coming to Amsterdam, Rembrandt lived and worked in the big house of Hendrick van Uylenburgh, who sold paintings for a living and also managed an art school. In this busy place, Rembrandt met Hendrick's cousin, Saskia van Uylenburgh. She came from a prominent family in Friesland, in the northern Netherlands. But now she was an orphan, the youngest of three sisters and four brothers. Rembrandt fell in love with her and asked her to marry him. The

Seldom did Rembrandt paint flowers. It was considered a highly specialized subject in his day. But for the crown of his bride, he pictured beautiful examples that would require a blooming season from early spring to late fall to produce a magical mix that only the wand of Flora, the goddess of flowers, could make possible. The largest flower is a tulip, new to Holland during Rembrandt's lifetime.

wedding took place in her hometown in 1634. She was twenty-one years old, and Rembrandt was twenty-eight.

Saskia quickly became Rembrandt's chief model. The year they were married, he painted her in an extravagant costume as Flora, the ancient Roman goddess of flowers, gardens, and spring. In mythology, Flora's husband gave her eternal youth, a gift that Rembrandt gave to Saskia through his brush.

Saskia's gown is a silvery gray-green color, and with her left hand she lifts its long train. The fold that results points toward her face. The billowing sleeve, with its stripes and brocade, is painted with the kind of detail that requires close examination. Its folds cascade down, then back up, pointing to Saskia's face and making it the center of attention again. Rembrandt blocked out most of the background with shadows, except for a plant near the lower right corner of the canvas. The back of Flora's dress is also darkened so that her long and luxurious brown hair can barely be appreciated. Even her staff is aimed away from the bright side of the painting. Rembrandt felt that Flora's bounty was best represented by her lavish costume, sweet face, and floral crown. He surrounded his model with darkness to emphasize these features and to eliminate everything else.

Flora's extravagant gown swells as it descends from its crossed bodice and clasped shoulders. Its billowing sleeve and lifted train seem to symbolize abundance as much as the flowers crowning her head do.

Belshazzar's Feast

A Scholarly Neighbor

Menasseh ben Israel, Rembrandt's neighbor, was one of the most learned teachers in the city's Jewish community. While Rembrandt was making an etched portrait of the rabbi, they had long conversations about the feast of Belshazzar, the topic the Jewish scholar was researching. When Rembrandt came to paint the subject, he asked his neighbor how to paint the Hebrew letters that were the dramatic part of the scene.

Nebuchadnezzar, king of the ancient empire of Babylonia, conquered Jerusalem and looted its temple. He carted most of the city's citizens to Babylon, his capital, along with the sacred vessels of silver and gold that the Jews used for their religious ceremonies. One of his captives was Daniel, a man known for his wisdom. When Nebuchadnezzar died, his son, Belshazzar, became king. On one particular occasion, Belshazzar invited one thousand guests to a banquet and used the silver and gold utensils from Jerusalem. As his guests drank from them, they irreverently praised the Babylonian gods of silver and gold. Suddenly, a hand mysteriously began to write on the plaster wall of the banquet chamber.

"Mene, Mene, Tekel, Upharsin"

The Bible reports that "the king's face changed . . . his limbs gave way, and his knees knocked together." He cried for his enchanters, wise men, and astrologers, but they could not read the strange words. The queen remembered Daniel and recommended him to the king. Daniel came,

scolded the king for desecrating the temple vessels, and read the words aloud: "Mene, mene, tekel, upharsin." Daniel said they meant that the king's days were numbered and his kingdom would be divided among his enemies. That very night, Belshazzar was killed.

Rembrandt painted the frightening and dramatic moment when the fingers are writing their mysterious message. He decided to show only four of Belshazzar's many guests and a flute player in the shadows, and to move in close to them and the king. From an imaginary place close to the ground—as though he were kneeling or sitting on a stool while he painted the

These Hebrew words are the names of weights or units of money, but in Arabic they can also mean "numbered, weighed, and divided." The divine message is painted yellow, surrounded by gray. Rembrandt knew that the right combination of dark and light colors can give a luminous effect.

But they cannot tell her, for they are speechless, recoiling from the mystery.

Familiar Gold Goblets and a Death Sentence
Rembrandt used Belshazzar's body to divide his painting into three sections: the area above Belshazzar's uplifted arm, the area between his arms, and the area behind him on the left. Each section has lively patterns of chiaroscuro. Above the king's arm, the fingers write the brilliant Hebrew letters on the wall, surrounded by a halo of light, then darkness. The letters are the brightest spot on the canvas and their brilliance falls on Belshazzar's back. Rembrandt used similar shapes for the king's turban and the miraculous oval of light behind the letters, perhaps to make it clear that the message is for the king. The woman in red and the grapes and figs on the edge of the table share the second section, along with the shadows under the king's arm. The four figures behind the king make up the third area. A source of illumination off to the left finds their faces in a room that otherwise is almost black with darkness. The same light falls onto the gold of the king's extraordinary cape and little crown.

scene—Rembrandt emphasized the dramatic postures of Belshazzar and the woman in red on the right. Even though she is viewed from behind, it is easy to imagine that she saw the apparition first, screamed in terror, then fixed her eyes to the wall. When the king leaps to his feet to find out what is wrong, he sees the words and the disembodied hand, terror filling his wide-open eyes. Just as the woman did, he lifts his arm to shield himself from the mysterious writing. The woman on the far left has yet to see what is wrong, and turns to her companions.

Rembrandt placed both goblets close to the king's hands, for his use of the sacred vessels displeased the God of Israel, and represented all the evil things for which he was punished with death. The words in the upper right corner of the painting are the king's death sentence.

Rembrandt placed fur, a heavy gold brocade, and a gold wine jug close to one another, demonstrating his mastery of rich textures. These are created from ordinary brown, black, gray, yellow, and white paint, even the metallic effects.

Anslo and His Wife

"Counterfeits" for Everyone

Portraits hung on the walls of almost every Dutch house. Sometimes called "counterfeits," they were expected to look exactly like the persons depicted. Portraits came in various formats. Those that showed only the head were the most affordable kind. Other, larger paintings showed the face, the torso, and both hands. This was the type usually requested by Rembrandt's wealthier clients. Double portraits, which featured two people, showed the subjects standing or sitting, and required a large room with a high ceiling to be shown off well. Since even the houses of the wealthy were often too small for them, double portraits were not common. During his career, Rembrandt painted many portraits of individuals, but less than a half dozen double portraits. They presented a challenge he always loved. He had to find ways to show feelings between the two subjects, or they would appear wooden and detached on canvas.

"Paint Cornelis's Voice!"

The Mennonite minister Cornelis Claeszoon Anslo was known as an eloquent preacher and religious writer. His sect, named after a Dutchman, Menno Simons, actually began in Switzerland around 1525, but blossomed in the Netherlands during the lifetimes of Rembrandt and Anslo. The Mennonites looked to the words of the Bible to guide their lives in all things and accepted no other authority. Honest and hardworking, they made good neighbors and their religion appealed to Rembrandt. He must have learned a great deal about the Mennonite way of life when he prepared a series of portraits of Anslo in 1640 and 1641. Two drawings, an etching, and a painting resulted from their time together. A famous Dutch poet had urged Rembrandt to "paint Cornelis's voice." He said that Anslo's appearance was not important, and advised that "if you want to see Anslo, you have to hear him." Of course, a voice cannot be painted in a literal way, but it is possible to paint a man preaching.

It was the custom of Mennonite ministers to preach to their families at home. Rembrandt decided to make this the theme of his painting. In the double portrait the minister preaches to his wife, Aeltje. The gesture of his left hand is one that artists have used since ancient Roman times to signify that a man is an orator. As Aeltje carefully listens, she does not look at her husband, but toward the Bible, the source of all his wisdom and inspiration. Rembrandt reserved

Still life, or the painting of inanimate objects, was one of the glories of Dutch art, so Rembrandt had many models around him for inspiration. Tabletop arrangements were the most common ones. In depicting the books, Rembrandt laid paint on thickly. When it was still wet, he scratched into it with the wooden tip of his brush to indicate the edges of pages.

the few touches of color in the painting for the faces of the Anslo couple, whose clothing, in contrast, is dark and subdued.

Dripping Wax and Quenched Wicks

The Bible dominates one half of the canvas. By placing it in strong light above the rich red of the Oriental rug that covers the table, Rembrandt made it compete for importance with his human subjects. Unlike all the other books in the room, it is open and placed high upon a stand, which isolates it as an object to be venerated.

In the double candlestand behind the Bible, one candle has burned down and the other stands ready for use. Because Rembrandt placed the tall candle so close to the Bible, it is certain to have a religious meaning.

Explanations of the symbolic meaning of ordinary objects such as candles could be found in emblem books, which were published in the sixteenth and seventeenth centuries. In the painting, the flame of the candles has been extinguished, which in emblem books is a warning that life and earthly pleasures will also be quenched with death.

On the candlestand is a pair of snuffing scissors, which were used for trimming, cleaning, and extinguishing candles. In Mennonite congregations, the errors of members of the flock were often corrected by the brotherly advice of others. In the richly complex world of emblem books, the wax that dribbles from the candle represents the errors of the soul, and the scissors stand for brotherly correction. Cornelis Anslo was a man of great learning, and Rembrandt was wise and knowledgeable about religion and art, so it is likely that they discussed the symbols to be used in the painting.

In Dutch art, husbands and wives were frequently shown facing one another in separate paintings that were hung on either side of a fireplace or a door. Double portraits, like this one, were rare.

The Night Watch

Citizen Soldiers

A Dutch poet of Rembrandt's day wrote, "When the country is in danger, every citizen is a soldier." That was the idea behind the militia, or civic guard companies, which trained citizens how to fight and shoot in case their city was attacked. Each company drilled in archery, the crossbow, or the musket. By Rembrandt's time, militia companies were as much social clubs as military organizations.

Captain Frans Banning Cocq, out to impress everyone, chose Rembrandt to paint his militia company, with members of the company paying the artist to have their portraits included in the painting. The huge canvas was to be hung in the new hall of the militia headquarters, where it would be seen at receptions and celebrations along with other militia paintings.

By the mid-seventeenth century, there were more than one hundred big militia paintings hanging in public halls in the important cities of the Netherlands. In all of these group portraits, the men were evenly lined up so that each face got equal attention, just as they had been in traditional anatomy lesson paintings. Rembrandt did not like this way of presenting the scene. He had seen militia companies in action, and there were always people milling about who were not militiamen but who took part in their exercises and parades. To add realism to the piece, he decided to include some of these people, as well as a dog. There was room on the wall for a canvas about sixteen feet wide, large enough for Rembrandt to do what no other painter had ever done before. His idea was to show the exciting commotion before a parade began.

Two Handsome Officers

Everywhere in the painting, Rembrandt used sharp contrasts of dark and light. Everything that honors the citizen soldiers and their work is illuminated; everything else is in shadow. Captain Frans Banning Cocq is the man dressed in black with a red sash under his arm, striding forward in the center. Standing next to him is the most brightly lighted man in the painting, Lieutenant Willem van Ruytenburgh, attired in a glorious gold and yellow uniform, silk sash, soft leather cavalry boots, and a high hat with white ostrich plumes. His lancelike weapon, called a partisan, and the steel gorget around his neck—a leftover

The Night Watch was the largest and most ambitious commission in Rembrandt's life. No one had ever organized so many portraits into so lively and dramatic a composition. That some were better lighted than others was probably forgiven, because the painting brilliantly captured the volunteer militia's patriotic spirit and readiness to defend Amsterdam.

from the days when soldiers wore full suits of armor—are the only hints that he is a military man. Rembrandt links him to Banning Cocq by contrasting the colors of their clothing and by painting the shadow of Banning Cocq's hand on the front of van Ruytenburgh's coat. The captain is giving orders to his lieutenant for the militia company to march off.

Banning Cocq is dressed in a black suit against a dark background, yet he does not disappear. Rembrandt made him the most important person in the composition. Van Ruytenburgh

Captain Frans Banning Cocq, the man in black wearing the red sash, was the commander of one of Amsterdam's volunteer civic guard companies. Here he commands his lieutenant, Willem van Ruytenburgh, to march off with the soldiers. His order may have been followed by a few uplifting words, for the captain's hand is held in a gesture of oratory. Rembrandt imbued both men with looks of great intelligence and purpose, to set a tone for the entire composition.

turns to listen to him, which shows his respect for his commander. Banning Cocq's face stands out above his bright red sash and white collar. How well Rembrandt knew that darkness makes faces shine! The captain's self-assured pace, the movement of the tassels at his knees, and the angle of his walking staff are proof of the energy and dignity of his stride.

Muskets and Mascots

On either side of these two handsome officers, broad paths lead back into the painting. Rembrandt knew that when the huge group scene was placed above eye level on the wall of the militia headquarters, these empty areas would be the first to be seen. He wanted them to lead the eyes of viewers to figures in the painting who did not have the advantage of being placed in the foreground. In the middle of one of these paths is a man in red pouring gunpowder into the barrel of his musket. Behind the captain, only partially seen, another man shoots his gun into the air, and a third militiaman, to the right of van Ruytenburgh, blows on his weapon to clean it. Loading, shooting, and cleaning were part of the standard drill for musketeers, and so they were included in the painting to demonstrate the men's mastery of their weapons.

Walking in a stream of bright light down the path on the left is a blond girl dressed in yellow with a dead chicken tied to her waist. She has a friend in blue behind her. In their public shows, the militia would choose two young girls

To prepare for a shooting exercise, this man pours gunpowder into his musket.

This militiaman blows firing powder from his weapon to clean it.

35

to carry the emblems of their company, here the claws of a bird. The yellow and blue of the girls' costumes are the militia's colors. In the parade that is being organized, these mascots will take a prominent place, the fair-haired girl holding aloft the chicken's claws.

Eighteen men each paid Rembrandt one hundred guilders or more to paint their portraits in The Night Watch, *but this young girl, a sort of mascot, is more brightly lit than most of them. Like all children of the time, she is dressed as an adult, but in old-fashioned clothes. The bright light that picks her out from the men is proof that this is not a night scene.*

Many of the background figures stand on stairs so that their faces can be seen. The man above the girl in yellow is Jan Corneliszoon Visscher, after Banning Cocq and van Ruytenburgh the highest-ranking person in the militia company. He waves a flag that combines the colors of the militia company with the three black crosses of Amsterdam. While Rembrandt did not pose him in bright light, he made him important by placing him high up on the stairs, by showing the sheen in his costume, and by giving him the large flag to unfurl.

A Red Ribbon and Fine Old Clothes
In spite of his partial appearance, the drummer on the right seems ready to come forward to lead a march with his staccato beat. The sound seems to bother the dusty dog below. Behind the drummer, two men appear to be figuring out their places in the formation. The one in the white collar and black hat outranks many of the others in the scene. His prestige is signaled in an unusual way: A red ribbon dangles over his head, tied to the lance of the man in armor behind van Ruytenburgh. Additional lances can be counted in the darkness, some leaning against the wall, others carried by militiamen. Their crisscross patterns add to the feeling of commotion that Rembrandt has captured everywhere on the huge canvas.

The costumes worn in this group portrait are much more ornate and colorful than what Dutchmen ordinarily wore every day. Some, like the breeches and helmet of the man shooting his musket behind Banning Cocq, go back a hundred years to the beginnings of the militia company. In the eyes of many Dutchmen, clothing associated with a glorious past brought special dignity to the company. What an opportunity for Rembrandt, perhaps the greatest lover of old clothes in Amsterdam!

Not a Night Watch

"Night Watch" is a mistaken title that was given to the painting over a hundred years after Rembrandt died, but it has stuck, and is what the painting is almost universally called. Although the exaggerated chiaroscuro does give an impression of nighttime, there is daylight in the scene. It comes from the left, as the shadows under Banning Cocq's feet prove. And it is clear that no one in the painting is on watch, alert to the approach of an enemy. The official title of the painting is *Officers and Men of the Company of Captain Frans Banning Cocq and Lieutenant Willem van Ruytenburgh.*

Rembrandt completed the painting in 1642, when he was thirty-six years old. He probably had no idea that it would be the most famous Dutch painting of all time. In 1678, one of his former students wrote that it would "outlive all its rivals," and within another century the painting was considered one of the wonders of the world.

Jan Corneliszoon Visscher was the highest-ranking militiaman after Banning Cocq and van Ruytenburgh.

Rembrandt's contemporaries recognized that this man's helmet and most of the armor and costumes of the other men in the painting had not been in style for over a hundred years. Wearing fine, old, well-cared for armor and handsome costumes of a bygone time showed one's respect for tradition. The antique armor also commemorated the era when the militias were first founded.

Aristotle with a Bust of Homer

Remembering Great Men

As a youth, Rembrandt learned Roman history and the epic poems of the Greeks. When he began to earn money from his paintings, he spent a small fortune on busts of Roman emperors and Greek philosophers. One was of Homer, the Greek storyteller and poet, whose bust is probably the one seen in this painting. Although there are more questions and mysteries about the great poet's life than facts and details, the one fact all writers do accept is that Homer was blind.

Aristotle Contemplates the Bust of Homer

Aristotle lived five hundred or more years after Homer, and in Holland, outside of the characters from the Bible, he was the best known of all the ancients. Rembrandt showed the great teacher with his hand on top of a bust of Homer. Aristotle looks as though he has been studying the poet's face, and now stares off into the distance. His contemplative mood seems fitting for a philosopher. All of Aristotle's study was based on seeing and experiencing things first-hand; perhaps he wonders how Homer could depict life and nature so truthfully in his poems without seeing what he described. But the theme of the painting certainly is not blindness; it is about the gift of inner vision.

Linking Three Great Men

Aristotle's face is framed in black and glows as much as the chain he wears and the marble top of Homer's head. The philosopher's black tunic acts like the pedestal that supports Homer's head.

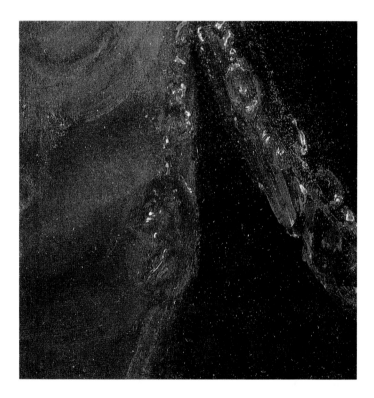

The legendary emperor and general Alexander the Great had been Aristotle's student. Here he is commemorated in the medallion that hangs from Aristotle's heavy chain. Alexander is pictured in profile as rulers were on coins.

To emphasize that Homer was blind, Rembrandt kept direct light off his face. Homer's fame is based on two epic poems. The Iliad *is about the exciting last days of the Trojan War, while* The Odyssey *recounts the adventures of Odysseus on his way home from the war.*

Suspended from the gold and silver chain is a medallion with a portrait of Aristotle's most famous pupil, Alexander the Great. The chain cascades to the philosopher's left hand, and then the sleeve leads back to his face, while the other sleeve links Aristotle to Homer. The creamy color of the marble bust is repeated throughout the sleeve, further connecting the men. The light that bathes Aristotle's face and sleeves does not fall upon Homer's blind eyes. Rembrandt emphasizes the bust by placing it on a table covered with red cloth.

Jacob Blessing the Sons of Joseph

Witnessing the Blessing

Rembrandt painted the biblical patriarch Jacob at the end of his life blessing his grandsons Ephraim and Manasseh. The blessing took place while Jacob's family was living in Egypt. Joseph, the children's father, was a very great lord there, so Rembrandt has crowned his head with a turban.

Asenath, the daughter of an Egyptian priest, was Joseph's wife and the mother of Ephraim and Manasseh. Aside from her jewelry and tall hat, nothing suggests her elevated station in Egyptian society. Rembrandt dressed her in a plain brown gown that almost blends with the background, but the shadow behind her left arm seems to push her forward.

The three generations of males are arranged in the shape of a triangle, their figures leaning toward one another with affection and respect. Asenath stands outside of this group, but a red blanket stretches from Jacob to her. This ruby-colored field links her closely to the boys and men, as does her tender look of love. Rembrandt filled two sides of the canvas with large swags of drapery. The biblical characters, who fill most of the remaining space, are concentrating on only one thing: the blessing. All eyes watch Jacob's fingers touch Ephraim's head. To heighten the importance of this act, Rembrandt placed Jacob's fingertips in the middle of the canvas.

Blessings and Tricks

As a boy, Jacob had cheated his older brother out of his blessing. Jacob's mother, Rebekah, helped Jacob disguise himself as his brother. It was easy because his father was blind. Although the brother had hairy arms and Jacob's were smooth, all Jacob had to do was wear the skins of young goats like gloves. When Isaac felt the skins, he was sure he was blessing his oldest son.

Jacob wears an animal skin draped across his shoulders as a reminder of the skins. He knows he should be blessing Joseph's older son, Manasseh; that was the custom. Instead, his hand is on the blond head of the younger, Ephraim. Joseph gently reaches under his father's arm to guide his fingers to Manasseh's head, but to no avail. Instead, the patriarch assures Joseph that both boys will be great, but that Ephraim will be the greater of the two.

The brown swags of drapery flanking this painting force the sacred figures into closer intimacy by reducing the space on the canvas. The left one echoes Jacob's posture as he blesses his grandson. The one on the right seems to reinforce the dignified posture of Asenath, mother of the boys, who stands next to her husband, Joseph.

Self-Portrait

Painted with Mirrors

Rembrandt turned to his own face as a subject for his paintings again and again. From his youthful days in Leiden to his last years in Amsterdam, he made almost one hundred self-portraits, some of them etchings and drawings, but more than half of them paintings. He was the first artist in history to memorialize his own image so often, and few after him painted their faces with as much diligence. Only his countryman, the nineteenth-century artist Vincent van Gogh, made the self-portrait as important a subject.

Rembrandt left no diaries and few letters, and his contemporaries jotted down none of his words. The self-portraits are his autobiography, telling frankly of his early self-confidence and success, and his eventual disappointment and sadness.

Avoiding Symmetry

In 1660, Rembrandt painted this self-portrait, in which he depicts himself with furrows across his

Being his own model involved a clever arrangement of mirrors. Rembrandt probably used two of them. The first one reversed his image, as all mirrors do. The second one reflected the image from the first mirror, reversing it back to normal. It was located so Rembrandt could see himself exactly as he is in the portrait.

forehead and eyebrows arched. If the expression suggests displeasure at what he saw in the mirror as he copied himself, the jaunty angle of his large black beret signals the will to make the portrait an imposing one, no matter what the painter was thinking about at the moment.

The slope of the hat also prevents the right and left sides of the canvas from being mirror images of each other. Rembrandt did not like symmetry, so to avoid it further here, he turned his body and head slightly. The beret casts gentle shadows on the right side of the artist's face, but the most important shadows in the painting are behind Rembrandt, between his shoulders and hat. Although they are in the background, they keep Rembrandt from looking as if he is standing against the wall.

Rembrandt's upturned collar and hat isolate his face from the background. He painted the tip of his nose at a point the same distance from the top, left side, and right side of the canvas, marking it with a dab of white paint to show that bright light was shining on it and to make it all the more noticeable. The gray shadow of his beard and the mass of gray, brown, and white hair give a candid impression of his aging.

Woman with a Pink

Unconventional Beauty

As Rembrandt approached the end of his life, a couple asked him to paint their portraits. The names of these intriguing people are not known today, or anything about them except what can be seen in their portraits. Their clothes are more theatrical than the normal garments of Amsterdamers and perhaps had a special meaning. But behind their unconventional exteriors, Rembrandt saw a quiet strength and inner beauty that inspired him to paint two of his most appealing portraits.

More Precious Than Pearls

The husband has reaching, soulful eyes and a handsome face. But his wife's portrait is more interesting because of a revealing contradiction between her wealth and her manner. Her ornate dress and jewelry of gold and pearls are showy, yet she seems totally untouched by their richness. While Rembrandt painted the folds and puffs of each rosette on her dress and the gleam of every pearl across her head, they seem to be here only to emphasize her face and the flower held between her fingers. A painting framed in gold in the background directs no attention to itself but instead calls attention to the woman's eyes. Rembrandt also positioned the tip of his subject's nose exactly in the middle of the top portion of the canvas, just as he had done with his own nose in a self-portrait. The woman's face, with its kind and inward expression, is the subject of the painting. Her head gently nods toward the

MAN WITH A MAGNIFYING GLASS

Rembrandt mysteriously created the impression of space between this quietly beautiful woman and the wall behind her. He decided not to use diagonal lines, or a shadow from her body, the usual ways to separate a sitter from the background. Instead, he surrounded her with atmosphere, something more difficult to paint than any face.

45

carnation, or pink, in her right hand; perhaps this flower is a clue to what is behind her dreamy look.

In portraits of married couples at the time, pinks were a symbol of faithfulness. When a man and a woman became engaged, each was painted holding a pink, and the portraits were exchanged. Rembrandt's ingenious way of showing both the woman's wealth and her deep feelings toward her

husband is a kind of parable. He is stating that fidelity is more precious than pearls. The magnifying glass in the husband's hand might be a parallel symbol meaning that as close as one looks—even through a magnifying glass—no fault can be found in his wife.

The touching love between the man and woman must have moved Rembrandt deeply. Never had he lavished as much attention on a portrait of a woman since painting Saskia, dead now for almost thirty years. Their son, Titus, married the daughter of one of Rembrandt's friends at about the time Rembrandt was painting the portraits of the couple, a union that must have furthered Rembrandt's interest in symbols of marital happiness and fidelity. But Titus died before the first anniversary of his wedding, and on October 4, 1669, Rembrandt followed him.

Rembrandt's last years were filled with disappointments, sadness, and financial woes. Toward the end of his life, he declared bankruptcy, and was forced to sell his house, and his collections of costumes, books, ancient sculptures, and paintings. Although respected and still in demand, Rembrandt's painting style fell out of fashion with the new generation of patrons, and many important portrait commissions went to younger artists.

No matter how sad Rembrandt's final years became, he could always be proud that many of his greatest paintings were still bringing him fame. They hung on the walls of Amsterdam's public buildings, which were the art museums of his day. What he did not know was that his fame would continue unbroken for more than three hundred years. Today all of Rembrandt's works bring pleasure to art lovers, not just his famous paintings but his private self-portraits and even quickly made sketches on scraps of paper. His personality dominates all of them like the light that comes from the shadows in his paintings.

THE THREE TREES

What Makes a Rembrandt

Rembrandt used chiaroscuro, the intense contrast of light and dark, to create dramatic effects.

1.

2.

3.

4.

1. Light illuminates the men's faces and white collars and the books on the table, while dark shadows hide unnecessary details.

2. The only bright color is red.

3. The men are posed informally.

4. The faces are portraits of individuals.

a Rembrandt?

THE SYNDICS OF THE CLOTHMAKERS' GUILD